Library of Congress.

Cataloging-in-Publication Data Av

Published in 2021 by Somatic Thera
PO Box 245, San Geronimo, CA 94965.

Copyright © 2021 Cara Gereau. All Rights Reserved.

Cover and Illustrations by Zoe Saunders.

Edited by Jennifer Rees.

No part of this book can be reproduced in any form or by written, electronic or mechanical, including photocopying, recording, or by any information retrieval system, without written permission from the author.

ISBN: 978-0-578-95083-9

For
Juliette and Grace

Today was going to be the best day ever.
Claire's friends had all mastered climbing the giant rope structure at the park. Claire so wanted to join them in their monkey swinging and screeching at the very top.

She had practiced and practiced with her mother and had finally made it to the top with ease!

When Claire arrived at the park with her mother, she could see her friends playing, and her hands tingled with excitement.

They were at the top of the giant spider-like climbing structure! "YES!" she thought, clapping her hands together. Claire felt her arms grow long as she imagined herself swinging from the ropes with her monkey friends.

Claire's mom opened the door, and Claire leapt out, letting out a few monkey sounds. But, first, where was Peck Peck?
Claire looked inside her bag.

"No!" Claire whispered. "Peck Peck isn't here!"

"Mama," said Claire softly. "Mama." But Claire's mother wasn't listening; she was already talking to another mother.

Claire looked in the car.
Peck Peck, her favorite stuffed penguin, wasn't there, either.

"Mama!" Claire said, this time a bit louder.

"Come on, sweetheart," Claire's mother said, "come and play with your friends."

Claire scrunched her face up, thinking. She wanted Peck Peck!

Claire looked at her mother and her friends.
She also wanted to play in the park!

"Mama!" Claire called, louder this time.

"What is it, honey?" her mother finally asked.
Just then, her mother's phone rang, and she turned her attention away from Claire to answer it.

Claire felt a terrible, burning, churning, ROARING fire in her throat.

The smoke billowed from her nose and mouth as she fumed and puffed and stomped her feet.

Her mother's eyes widened.

"Sweetheart, can we see Peck Peck after the park? Our friends are waiting."

"Noooooooooooo!"

Claire puffed and roared and ran back to the car, grunting the whole way.

"Ok, ok, we will go get Peck Peck," Claire's mother said.

Claire was silent as they pulled away from the park.
She saw her friends and some parents looking back at the car.

Her angry dragon melted away and her shoulders dropped as she noticed how embarrassed she was by her roaring and stomping. Tears started to fall. Claire felt like she was getting smaller and smaller. She had no words, and the only sounds she could make came out like soft mews as she cried.

The car pulled into their driveway,
and Claire's mother joined her in the back seat.
"I'm so sorry, Claire!"

Claire felt confused by all her feelings and hid her face from her mother.

"Oh, sweetheart, I'm sorry. You needed me to hear that you were upset! I know that you tried to keep it all in, but you really needed Peck Peck, and I had trouble listening."

Claire turned her head back toward her mother.
"I'm so sorry, Claire, can you forgive me?"
Claire looked at her mother's sad face and kind eyes and felt her own sadness leaving.

Her small kitten body felt like it was bigger and braver.
"I will try to do a better job listening," her mother whispered.
Claire felt her heart beam with love for her mother.

Claire leapt into her mother's lap and nuzzled her mother's shoulder.

"I'm sorry I yelled and made us go back home for Peck Peck. Do you forgive me?" Claire's mother wrapped her arms around her.

"Sweetheart, when we don't feel heard, our feeling parts let us know.

Your monkey part was so excited to play but then went away when you realized you forgot Peck Peck.

Your dragon part is fierce and strong and told me you were very angry about my not listening to you."

"And your kitten part told me that you were sad that we had a fuss and that you need me and love me.

I love your feeling heart and all your feeling parts because I love all of you."

Claire swung around her mother's back and placed her arms around her neck in a gentle hug. Her mother laughed in surprise.

Claire whispered into her mother's ear, "I love your feeling heart and all your feeling parts, too." Claire and her mother returned to the park with Peck Peck, who sat proudly in Claire's lap.

Claire clapped her hands together when she saw her friends were still on the giant climbing structure.

"Watch this, Peck Peck!" Claire whispered.
"I'm going to be the best monkey you have ever seen."

Claire swung from rope to rope, smiling at her friends as she climbed to the very top of the play structure.

Claire looked down to see if her mother was watching.
"Wow! I see you!" her mother said, smiling big.

Claire smiled back, her heart warm and happy.

An eruption of monkey calls filled the park.
Even Peck Peck seemed to smile. It was a really great day.

Cara Gereau is a wife, mother, and coach who lives in California. Cara has a MA in Somatic Counseling Psychology and her passion is supporting individuals and families so that they may gain more self-compassion, understanding and connection.

Made in the USA
Las Vegas, NV
28 August 2021